A COMMON GARMENT

A COMMON GARMENT

ANITA PATEL

RECENT
WORK
PRESS

A Common Garment
Recent Work Press
Canberra, Australia

Copyright © Anita Patel, 2019

ISBN: 9780648404262 (paperback)

A catalogue record for this book is available from the National Library of Australia

All rights reserved. This book is copyright. Except for private study, research, criticism or reviews as permitted under the Copyright Act, no part of this book may be reproduced, stored in a retrieval system, or transmitted in any form by any means without prior written permission. Enquiries should be addressed to the publisher.

Cover design: Recent Work Press from a photograph provided by Anita Patel
Set by Jasmine Braybrooks and Charlotte Anderson

recentworkpress.com

For Scott, Anil, Asha and Tarla
You hold my heart, you are my home ...

Contents

Onkaparinga	1
Geragok	3
out into her country ...	4
Surat udara	6
Raising Ravana	7
Tsunami	8
Navigating Gija country	9
Don't be afraid	10
Cooking rice	12
colours of her country	14
Peribahasa	15
Dia	16
Wajah/muka	17
Your voice	18
Across black water ...	19
Women's talk	21
Soul	22
Aunties	23
That's their story ...	25
Cane cutter's bride	27
Sita	28
Young woman washing dishes, 1882 (by Camille Pissarro)	29
Fried bread and mango juice	30
Apples and chillies	32
Common garment	33
So much fruit ...	34
Tau suan	35
Wearing red for Hanuman	36
Fold this day ...	38
In a gallery ...	39
Makan angin	40
Child's play	41
Greeting	42

Mr. Darwin's room	43
Spring day in Kingston	44
Poppies	45
Luminous miracles	46
Vighneshvara: Destroyer of obstacles	47
Nest	48
The last despair	49
In our great grandmother's room	50
Bereft	51
You would have loved the flowers ...	52
Family tree	53
Pontianak	54

Onkaparinga

Driving through Onkaparinga on an autumn afternoon
I remember the first time I saw this word:
On ka par in ga—the loveliness of it—
printed neatly in my school project
on Australian wool production ...
*I am a girl from an island of steamy sunshine where no one
has ever needed to wear wool*
But I copy down these woollen facts:
Sheep are sheared once a year
Wool is scoured in baths containing water, soap, and soda ash
Carding removes residual dirt and other matter left in the fibres
Our dining table is strewn with snips of coloured yarn,
pictures of merinos in dusty paddocks
and samples of fuzzy fabric from Onkaparinga
I am a girl from a land of coconut trees and rice fields
where sheep are non-existent
But I learn to savour these cosy words:
shearing, grading, scouring, carding, spinning, weaving,
worsted, twill, bobbin, fleece, spun yarn, jumbuck ...
They fold around my new heart—warm and snug
as a plaid rug (pale blue and pink) woven in Onkaparinga.
Today I discover that Onkaparinga
derives from the Kaurna word,
Ngangkiparinga (The Women's River)
I wish that I had known this—over four
decades ago when all that mattered was the fact
that this country rode to prosperity
on the sheep's back and Onkaparinga
was the place of looms and blankets
and my project had to be perfect because
I was not ...
I wish I had known that my love for Onkaparinga
(those splendid syllables)
was really a love for *Ngangkiparinga* ...

I wish that I had known this
because wool still prickles my tropical skin
but I am a woman who loves rivers ...

Geragok

Do you know the *geragok*?
Tiny shrimp
dried and beaten in the sun
with blood bright chillies—
a dash of this paste
will flavour a full bowl of rice
Geragok
Udang kering, cabai pedas
Ditumbuk lama, ditumbuk keras ...
And so they came
these milk skinned ghosts
blown over water in boats
as big as palaces
Siapa orang asing ini?
Kenapa mereka hendak ke sini?
Matanya biru sebagai gelombang
Dari mana mereka datang?
sarong squatting women with
frangipani eyes
and sailors from a far off land
pounded together
over centuries
and mingled in a bowl
of rice scented steam ...
lingering blaze on lips and tongue
scarlet sting of shrimp in rice
the heartbeat of a race echoing forever
in the *tumbuk buk buk*
of mortar and pestle ...

out into her country ...

At the John Flynn Hospital
in Alice Springs stolid ladies
offer us tea (included in the entry
price of $5 accompanied by an Arnott's
biscuit—Nice or Scotch Finger).
They dangle tea bags in thick mugs
at sunny tables covered
with prim perfect circles of lace ...
We wander through rooms
of yesteryear and examine small photos
of that good white doctor, John Flynn
(50 cents each—the same price for
floral decorated prayer cards)
the ladies lament the broken lock
and the ruined fence
(a constant problem due to the
high rate of youth crime).

In a room behind the kitchen—
with its wood fired stove and copper kettle—
an Arrernte woman shows us her paintings.
We see the buttocks and legs of her
people sitting flat on russet earth,
we see *Undoolya* Dreaming in a
flurry of vibrant dots ...

I got the right to put my art in this
white man's house ...
Outside on the verandah—voices
(old and young) chatter in unfamiliar words ...
The ladies hurry us along
They remind us that there is a church next door
and urge us to listen to godly music.
We leave the remainder of our

tea (now stone cold—
and pale as their skin)
and follow the Arrernte woman out
              into her country.

Surat udara

(Aerogramme)

Tucked between the covers
of a tattered exercise book—
a letter to my mother (your
daughter)
living in a country of snow and seasons:

28th Oct 64
My darling Yvonne,
I sent you the X'mas cake on Saturday 24th
Now do not be greedy and eat it before X'mas ...
There are some kachang cake in the box too ...
As soon as I feel fit I shall go down to town
and get you the ikan bilis,
Mr. Tay from the Supermarket promised that he would
get fresh stuff and pack them ready for shipment ...
I shall write the recipe for pineapple tart on the next page
so shall close with best love and kisses to one and all
Your loving Mum—

I see my mother's slim fingers
slitting the aerogramme
slowly, meticulously—taking care not to tear
the delicate blue of a faraway sky,
fearful of losing a single inky syllable ...

(*Surat Udara* with a map of Malaya on the stamp)
I see her in our tiny English kitchen
with the October sky falling like a leaden blanket
over the damp garden ...
I see her
holding the pale paper tenderly,
breathing in words from home ...

Raising Ravana

My father
raised Ravana
in papier mache glory—
gaudy painted
ten armed monster—
on guy ropes
in a Kenyan park

Ravana
three storeys tall
Ogre king of Alangka

and my father
a small boy—Hanuman
monkey smart and wily,
leaping from the walls of Langka
into the abyss of his future

setting fire to
his past with his tail.

Tsunami

Tsunami
such a pretty word
trips off
the tongue
in pleasing phonemes
(Japanese
—you know—
like sakura and
kimono).
Ink frilled waves
on fine rice paper:
an oriental image
as delicate as
porcelain
as elegant as
a tea ceremony.

Tsunami
The land rips
like ink washed paper
(pulped and shredded—
patterns dissolve)
and all those teacups
drop and shatter
spilling
precious liquid
in the sand.

Navigating Gija country

Gija artists map country
in unnameable
colours—scooped out of the earth,
scoured from stone,
blended, muddled and daubed
(charcoal, rust red, burnt orange,
ochre, olive, cream, muddy mauve,
pure white, honey yellow,
pale pink, black)
Gija country
(winkled out of soft rock
in an infinite palette of grainy pigments) ...
beehive hills, sandy riverbanks,
creek beds,
boabs, cycads, emu eggs,
pods, blossom, grass and
clouds, star spiked skies,
crocodile holes, *Woonggool*
the serpent leaving his trail
(white dots on black),
a line of chalk water, russet dirt—
unknown spaces—hung on white walls,
for us to traverse
as we navigate our way
into dreaming ...

Don't be afraid

(Jangan merasa takut)

Don't be afraid of this new sky—
the vast blue blast of it over our heads,
Jangan merasa takut
karena langit ini sama dengan langit
di mana-mana,
Don't be afraid because
it is the same sky everywhere.
Don't be afraid of girls named
Cheryl and Belinda flicking their blonde hair
and looking disdainfully at the contents of your lunch box.
One day their children will be trying to make
chilly sambal and *roti canai* on Masterchef.
Don't be afraid of new syllables,
scented with strawberry lip gloss
and vowels flattened like burst balloons,
Deadset as soon as you learn to speak Australian,
you're in like Flynn. It doesn't matter that
you look a bit different.
Don't be afraid of living secret lives,
Hidupan rahasia.
The one where you are a good daughter:
Anak patuh yang belajar baik-baik dan
masak nasi untuk makan malam,
Studying hard and cooking rice
for the evening meal,
And the one where you sashay down the street with your friends
in hotpants and a boob tube
keeping a look out for Asian aunties ...
Don't be afraid of the lurid pink icing on finger buns or of
eating a pie and sauce while you yearn for *sate ayam*.
Don't be afraid when coconut tanning oil,
on an Australian beach, starts to smell the same as *nasi lemak*
Or when you can't quite recall the *cicak* sound of geckoes

scurrying on the ceiling in your grandmother's house.
Don't be afraid when you're not sure if you prefer
a banana paddle pop or an *es kacang* on a hot day
Or when your memories fade like fallen rainbows ...
Don't be afraid because your heart is big enough to hold this new sky—
and your mouth will always know that the taste of
apples can never be the same as the taste of *rambutan.*
Jangan merasa takut
karena ingatan dan pelangi pasti kembali
setelah angin ribut,
Memories like rainbows will surely return after storms
Don't be afraid ...

Cooking rice

Nowadays—every Asian girl is given a rice cooker
for her wedding
The instructions are clearly printed
in a glossy pamphlet ...
This way we can make impeccable rice for
our families.
As I measure out the grains with precision
into a plastic cup (included for this purpose),
Dewi Sri the rice goddess wends her way through
padi fields—stepping
daintily among newly planted seedlings—
As I add water carefully (just enough),
Her naked feet splash in tepid
mud and ular sawah (rice padi snakes) slither
across her bare toes ...
As I sprinkle in the salt—a small pinch
but very necessary ...
She breathes sweetness into
pregnant grain (guarding the harvest)
poised on the petals of a lotus ...
As I cover the cooker and plug it into
the socket,
She sings the sacred rhythm of
Menanam, memanen—
that endless untranslatable cadence of
planting and harvesting, threshing and
winnowing, storing and cooking ...
a daily dance of life
from field to fire
As the rice bubbles and steams
in its electric prison,
I look for her muddy foot prints on my shiny
kitchen floor

As the rice cooks to pearly perfection
fluffy as a snow white cloud—just like
the picture in the brochure—
I listen for her voice and the quacks of
bebek paddling in the sawah
I listen ...
but all I hear is the click of a rice cooker
switching off—as a goddess topples
from her lipstick pink lotus into
a cardboard box, packaged neatly
next to a plastic measuring cup ...

colours of her country

I ask an Arrernte woman to name the colours of her
country. She looks at me bewildered.
We have just walked into the land of her
grandmother's birth—a place of soft green leaf,
terracotta rock, carmine earth (the dark ruby rust of it),
snow white bark, a breathtaking swipe of blue sky,
hard yellow figs waiting to darken
into deep sweet burgundy ...
She shows me the birthing cave high
above a sunlit shimmer of pale gold grass
This country hugs you, it knows you,
it talks to you ...
We step into wallaby tracks—feet and tails—
faintly marked in rosy dust
(our mob sit flat—bums on the dry earth,
digging sticks ready, or walk with our eyes
planted down, no use looking in the sky,
no tracks in the clouds)
I learn words for country (*apmere*), for
water (*kwatye*). I learn of *them old camel*
men, Afghan mob who stayed, became part
of Arrernte people, became part of the families.
I learn of Caterpillar Dreaming and *Undoolya,*
Eagle Dreaming. I see an old man's face carved
on weathered stone. I hear of spirits in the caves.
So I ask her again—to name the colours of her
country ... cerulean, scarlet, lemon, bronze, jade,
russet, sapphire, chocolate, cream, charcoal ...
No need for them words.
Them words don't make sense to us.
There is this dirt, these trees, this water, this sky ...

Peribahasa

(Proverb)

Spilt milk cannot be drunk
or scooped back into a cup
tapi nasi yang sudah menjadi bubur
masih bisa dimakan,
but rice which has become porridge
can still be eaten
and fills my mouth with
pearly softness
and the certainty of
kecap scented hope,
(enak dan hangat)
the taste of morning comfort
in my grandmother's
tropical kitchen ...
Later in my childhood
I will cry over milk
spilt on winter-hard asphalt—
an irretrievable white splatter
among shards of smashed glass,
I will cry because of angry voices
and because this milk
(unlike *hujan yang jatuh ke pasir*)
does not melt tenderly like rain into sand
but lingers maliciously in sticky trickles
on my shoes and books,
I will cry because this bottled milk
in a cold school yard is not a
bowl of fragrant *bubur*
waiting for me
in a kitchen far away ...

Dia

held carefully like fragile
eggs or glossy seeds in
a perfect bowl of three
letters—delicate
as a yoni,
conspicuous as a lingam—
three letters, two syllables,
one pronoun (personal
and possessive)—*dia*—
 this vessel
            cradles
the whole human race ...

Wajah/muka

Two words for face in my language:
Wajah from the Arabic *wajh*
rolls off the tongue
and melts like honey
in our mouths ...
Wajah—the cherished tenderness of
a human face ...
And yet ...
I prefer the honest drum beat
of *muka*. An ancient word
harvested from seas and
fertile earth, blown through palm fronds
and tossed about in monsoon rain—
coconut redolent thud of pestle in
mortar—*mu-ka* ...
hammer hard syllables
chiselling the naked face
of my Malay ancestors ...
When you lift the soft, saffron
silk mask of *wajah* ...
there is only *muka*.

Your voice

I riffle through your voice
in fragile pages of old Malay exercise books—
stained yellow as nicotine fingers—
Fry spice till you feel like sneezing
and when that first tickle comes
add asam, salt and kusum leaves then
mix together three teacups of second milk
from a freshly grated coconut
with ground chillies, onion and ginger
How much ginger? *Just one piece—the size*
of your thumb ...
No use pointing out that my thumb is
bigger than yours
or that I will be pulling ring tops
off cans of coconut milk
from an Australian supermarket ...
I will not be pounding spices in a
mortar and pestle—the buzz and whirr
of a coffee grinder has replaced
the dogged thump of stone on stone
in my kitchen—
but the faded ink of your voice speaks
long forgotten words (held somewhere
in my mouth and heart)—
bawang, blachan, serai, jintan—
nomadic syllables
wafting among the pots and pans—
sizzling the air with their fragrance ...

Across black water ...

On New Year's Eve in Vanuatu
I cook small, local crabs with you—
we buy them at Port Vila market—
a raffia tied fidgeting necklace
of carapaces and claws—
They crawl around in
the bathroom balefully ignoring
children's squeals and squirts of water ...
The sea snails that I purchased from
helpful women in cotton dresses
(offering advice
on how to prepare them)
are clamped shut and in the dust bin ...
You pile the crabs into the kitchen sink
and make an island dish of yams and greens
I chop eggplants, onions and chillies
to cook my mother's recipe for *brinjal
pachiri*—spicy, sweet and sour ...
We prepare a sauce of curry and coconut
to flavour these muddy, hard to clean
crustaceans
You are undaunted by the mayhem
and muddle of three generations of
foreigners in a holiday house ...
and we talk about your baby left
behind, with in-laws, on another island ...
how much you miss her small hands
and tight curls ...
We talk about our lives as women,
about fathers and husbands
and the non-ending work ...
At dinner time you join the clamour
at our table and I ask if you would rather
be at home—but you settle down,

comfortably, with a toddler on your lap,
and tell us about drunken, angry men
bashing on doors and demanding food
in the early hours—
We exchange kisses at the stroke of midnight
as New Year bops its way in
to the clatter and song of villagers
banging tins across black water ...

Women's talk

Have you noticed
how the purl and plain of
women's talk is tangled
and snarled
when a man enters the room?
Suddenly stitches are dropped
in the middle of a pattern
worked on for hours
and the cosy blend of colours
dark and light is
snagged and knotted
beyond repair.
The ropy twist
of mannish yarn
weaves its way
harsh and relentless
into the whispered silk
of confidences,
ruining the rich brocade
of spoken moments
(embroidered daintily
with truth and terror)
and the fine cobweb lace
of lies half told.
No deft fingers
can save the garment now
it falls
in a cambric crush
next to the broken loom—
the last threads hang loose
a ravelment of bombast
and vainglory.

Soul

*You have not earned the right
to use this word,*
a white professor said to the
Persian girl
as he ran his eye over her
poem. And filled with shame
(at her own presumption)
she scratched out four letters
that she had not earned
the right to use.
The word disappeared
along with her mother's laugh,
the sizzle of turmeric in a pan,
cool floors, lemon trees, the heat of
summer sand, a honey cake placed
tenderly into her mouth,
her heart dipping and lifting
like a wayward kite,
scoldings, kisses, anger, fright …
brushed away like messy crumbs
from a rich man's table …

Aunties

Fete day.
Balloon burst of sky
stretches bright over asphalt
and stalls spring up
(all the old favourites).
Chocolate wheel
in pride of place
under powder drifts of wattle blossom
sweet scented as coconut ice.
Always the same set up.
That's how we like it.
The mums' new permed
summer frocks swirling.
The dads in shirtsleeves
a squadron of megaphones.
The children everywhere
lolly-spittle sticky-lipped screaming.

An hour to the grand opening

and the aunties arrive
purple, saffron, peacock green
a gaudy flotilla,
kohl eyes flashing,
dupattas flying, sandals flapping
rapping out orders
as we follow behind.
They billow and jangle
—a rainbow tangle—
across the asphalt.
We slink along in hipster jeans
halter tops and platforms
and feel the eyes

(hard blue burning
bright like the Australian sky)

on our brown skinned backs.
'I'm bloody not serving their
stinking curry,' mutters the bravest of us
and we make a break for the lucky dip ...
An hour later munching on sauce soaked snags,
swinging on the arms of our Aussie mates,
pulling strings of spitty stick jaw sugar a foot

from our greasy gobs—

we notice a spicy waft of
vindaloo and kofta in the air ...
They are eating it everywhere
even the blokes from the sausage sizzle
and the blue rinsed lamington ladies.

Bangle brandishing ladle dipping
bazaar bantering,
the aunties dance gleefully—
sub continental witches stirring
their cauldrons.

That's their story ...

This strong wild woman, Kali,
whirls like fire through the universe
stamps on demons—fearlessly
does not feel the need to comb her hair
or straighten her skirt or powder her blue
black face,
This strong, wild woman
pokes her tongue out like a warrior
lets loose with words and weapons,
does not suffer fools gladly,
adorns herself
with a garland of skulls, rides a lion,
wields a sword, is the darkness from
which all things come, is the bringer and preserver
of life, this strong wild woman
free as her dishevelled flowing hair, blue as
the deepest ocean and the night sky,
wise as the wisest mother
this strong wild woman
(and here's the bit that I don't get)
stops her frenzied dance,
wipes her blood stained
feet and bows her head
because a supine man
said "Hey Kali, you're a bit
out of control,
You need to settle down ..."
Well that's the story that is put about
by Brahmin priests, anointing their
precious Shiva lingam with sacred oil
and saffron milk,
that's the story that they would have
you believe—these men with the
mark of Shiva on their foreheads

wagging their fingers in reproach
at stripes of red on temple walls
(red is the impurity of
women's blood, white is the purity
of semen)
that's their story—the wild woman
stopped dancing because she was
admonished by her husband
and she was ashamed ...
that's their story
but I'm just not buying it
no matter how many Shivas tell me
that it's true ...

Cane cutter's bride
(Museum of Fiji)

Suddenly you accost me
with silent sepia eyes—
a sallow smudge of newsprint
hidden among weapons and bones.
You shrink and flutter
like a frightened bird
    trapped
in the crimson mesh
of your wedding sari.
I am caught
in your dark gaze
in the tattered trace
of hands and face:
ragged remnants
of a fragile gift
carefully wrapped
and dispatched
with good wishes
to an alien land.

Sita

Sita—when you followed
your blue skinned lover
along tangled forest paths
Did he marvel at your fearless laughter
filling the darkness with hope?
Did his heart lift at the sight of you,
his sure-footed wife
marching melodically into the wilderness
on bell garlanded feet?
Did he realise that this was your place?
the biting green of vine and leaf
the howl of creatures still unknown
the damp earth beneath your feet
the sweet familiar breath of home.

Sita—did you dance into a hoop of flames
holding your painted hands before your face?
Did he weep as the fire wrapped you
in its silken embrace?
And you cried out for the shade of a fig tree
and the fragrance of rain beaten earth …
Did he watch as you stepped out of ashes
shaking embers from your hair?
Did he hear you call upon your mother
to open her arms and clasp you to her heart?
Did he witness your leap into the abyss?

Sita—pure as the morning—born in a furrow
Falling, unafraid, into black endlessness …

Young woman washing dishes, 1882
(by Camille Pissarro)

Soft and solid
the dip and curve
of a woman
washing dishes
draws a crowd
of tourists in loud
T-shirts and scruffy
art students.
We jostle each other
to see her better—
this rosy girl in
French sunshine—
and she ...
unmindful of the mob,
steadily completes the job,
rinsing the last
plate carefully.

Fried bread and mango juice

for my grandmother, Suraj Ba

My father bought mangoes
(a dozen or so)
and we carried them home
in a gunny sack
filled with the dark
orange smell of ripeness—
my five-year-old mouth watered
as my father slapped the sack
down in front of my mother.
Her face did not change at the
sight of the fruit (now a bit sticky
and blackened in places,
sap seeping slowly through
small splits in the tender skins)
these were not the mangoes
she expected,
firm and smooth—ready to eat
in neat, sweet slices—
Yet her eyelids did not flicker
at this messy offering
and I watched as she
washed the sack carefully,
peeled each soft fruit
and rubbed the yellow flesh
on harsh hessian
till her knuckles grew red and raw
and the thick juice flowed
like a honeyed miracle—
enough to fill a pitcher and then some more—
And after that she rolled dough
into silky discs, slipped them
into sizzling oil
and lifted out *puris*—
small, golden balloons ...

I have had eight decades of eating
and now my dry mouth tastes nothing—
but in the stillness of my dreams
I feast like a child
on fried bread and mango juice ...

Apples and chillies

Last night I heard a woman talk about apples—
like fragrant orbs hung in the twilight,
the crunch and tang of apple stories
beguiled us for a while ...
But I must admit I do not relish this cold climate fruit—
Fine for fairy tales and picnic baskets—
rosy sweet, neatly sliced, baked in a pie,
delicious, no doubt, but too cosy
for those of us who grew up with the
scarlet spite of chillies on our tongues—
those shiny, pointed (sharp as painted
fingernails) berries spiking our taste buds
and staining our lips blood bright ...
There is no place for crisp and juicy
apple simple syllables in mouths that know
the seductive malevolence of chillies ...

Common garment

In the candy pink hush
of this room—we gather around
a table scattered with teacups,
scruffy magazines and an
unfinished jigsaw puzzle ...
On the television Cyclone Debbie
wreaks havoc—palm trees bend in half,
waves crash, dark skies split open.
We watch the catastrophe
unfold in this pastel space of
women's voices ...
Unified by our common garment
(pink and white)
our fingers stretch out to
the warm campfire of each other's
stories ...
The skins of normal lives hang
limp in small cubicles—we have shed them
for these long hours together,
wrapped softly in a cowl of
words and waiting—
Cyclone Debbie tantrums her way
across beaches and townships—
demolishing, obliterating,
annihilating ...
In this still place of
shared laughter, beating hearts
and naked breasts,
we gaze at the swirling
violence of a distant disaster ...

So much fruit ...

for a Malaysian Grandmother in Australia

You look so odd in this backyard
(for it is a backyard not a garden)
with its dusty lawn and barbeque,
long unused, lurking in the corner.
Surrounded by the splintery teeth
of a paling fence, you pause
under a tree purple heavy
with fruit.
Later in the kitchen your deft fingers
dance like butterflies—
wielding a pair of chopsticks in
a sizzling wok—conjuring the perfume
of a time long gone.
I show up at your door each afternoon
(sticky-lipped, licking a banana paddle pop).
We step out among plums
split and syrupy, scattered on dry grass—
What to do with so much fruit?
This question never plagued you
when *rambutans* clustered,
crimson and fragrant,
in leafy branches on the tree
in your garden at home.

Tau suan

(Sweet soup)

Split mung beans
and rock sugar boiled into hot soup,
mingled with the scent of Elizabeth Arden
and a whiff of Sobranie
cigarettes, *tau suan* bought in a tin
from a lantern lit stall
and spooned sweetly
into my sleepy mouth at midnight ...
After the shimmer and sparkle of
cheong sams, saris and silken frocks,
cocktails, flirty chit-chat
and pretty faces vying
for a favourable verdict
from the mirror on the wall ...
tau suan brought home carefully
for a sleeping eight year old
waiting in the darkness
for the crunch of *yoo char kway*
in *pandan* fragrant syrup and the smell
of her mother's fancy cigarettes ...

Wearing red for Hanuman

On Tuesdays I wear red to work—
not my favourite silk *kameez*,
or a vermillion spot on my forehead
or a scarlet bloom in my hair ...
I wear a crimson scarf or jacket or
skirt or stockings ...
apparel that will not catch the eye,
something unnoticeable,
and they never notice because
I am a good worker—my reports are
meticulous, my calculations perfect,
I chat with my colleagues, I don't
question my superiors, I deliver on
time ... so no one observes that I don't
eat anything at staff morning tea on
sacred Tuesdays *(Mangalvar Vrat)*
dedicated to fasting for Lord Hanuman—
no food from dawn to dusk
for the betterment of health,
victory over enemies and to reduce
bad effects caused by the planet Mars—
Tuesday is a day to wear red for Hanuman
in this—pleasant enough—office
where Emma and Gemma share
blonde secrets and the men argue
about last night's Rugby match—
These people are very nice to me ...
the women remark upon my thick plait
(so black and shiny)
and my skin—*that beautiful brown*—
and my quickness with numbers—*an Indian talent* ...
Sometimes they ask me where to get the
best curry in town or for a good vindaloo recipe ...
How to explain that my

Bengali family has never eaten vindaloo
(a Goan specialty)?
How to tell them that I started my morning
with prayers to an elephant headed god and
I am fasting to honour a monkey deity today?
How to tell them that, on rainy days
in this cold city,
I yearn for my mother's cardamom chai,
the smoky smell of sandalwood *agarbatti*
and freshly fried *poha* fragrant with
turmeric, curry leaves and mustard seeds?
How to tell them that tonight we will
eat a meal of wheaten bread and *jaggery*
(no salt) because this is the correct
way to break our *Mangal* fast?
On Tuesdays I wear red to work,
politely decline a sausage roll, generously share
a vindaloo recipe
(from the Australian Women's Weekly)
and hand in my flawless calculations ...

Fold this day …

Fold this day tight
and hold it close—
hide it in your pocket
or handbag or under your shirt,
wrap it in tissue,
squash it in your purse …
this tiny bright wad of day
when the sun was just warm enough,
the air just still enough,
the clouds—a feather scud
(flitting across eternal blue) …
this day of picnic rugs, straw hats
and sandals flung carelessly
and a girl in orange shorts
walking on rain damp grass
and the trees that luminous, grateful
green, this wattle dazzled day
yellow buttered with light
and ducks paddling on
pewter water
and children tossing crumbs
and birdsong rustling branches …
      this day—fold it tight
      (over and over again)
      and hold it …

In a gallery ...
for Scott

In a gallery, we separate
instinctively, you walk slowly
and stop in front
of each piece—examining
the canvas or sculpture carefully—
painstaking, thorough,
needing to know ...
I skitter around like
a magpie in a jewellery shop,
choosing a face, a colour, a shape,
a tiny adornment to hide away in
my nest of treasures ...
Later we meet again, over
tea—two pots of English Breakfast
and a piece of cake to share—
(sometimes my choice,
sometimes yours)
You generously
offer details and opinions
about all the art that I raced
past and ignored
in my urge to glean
the brightest trinkets ...
and I rummage in my nest
for a few sparkly baubles to
share with you ...

Makan angin
(Eating the air)

I eat the air of
my cold city,
frost flavoured
mouthfuls of
high country blueness,
Saya makan angin di kota ini,
(Angin yang terdingin)
Bagaimana rasanya?
Tanpa bau kelapa
atau harum melati,
No hint of coconut,
or jasmine in the
frozen breeze—
and my feet
scrunch through damp drifts of
brown and gold
beneath a pattern of bare branches,
Pasir panas dan sawah hijau
pun tidak ada di sini ...
Tapi saya senang berjalan
di tepi danau terang
sebagai kaca bening ...
Makan angin
di kota dingin,
No hot sand or green rice fields
in this place ...
But I am joyful
walking by a glass lake ...
eating the air
of my cold city.

Child's play

for Anil, Asha and Tarla

Remember the hard smooth flame
of rubber seeds—
between our small palms
(we loved that pure heat
as only children can) ...
rubbing fire into
rubber seeds and hoarding
scarlet beads fallen
from the saga tree—
shiny stones in treasured piles
next to timid leaves
of touch me not—opening
and closing with each
brush of our fingers ...
Earlier in a cold land I
tipped acorns out of tiny
eggcups, cracked conkers
watched sycamore pods whirl
like helicopters in the autumn breeze ...
and in a life to come
my own children will peel
soft paper from the trunks
of eucalypts, gather gumnuts sticky
with minty scent, scoop tentacles
out of rock pools on antipodean
beaches and watch time float
backwards and forwards in
a single puff of air blown strong
and bright ...
as the seeds of a dandelion
drift gently out of sight ...

Greeting

Driving home through
freshly laundered country
wrung out and tipped in
folds of green on green
under an upturned washing basket
of pale blue sky ...
we snuggle cosily into a view
of undulating mossy brightness,
soft and muddled like quilt covers
rolled up after winter,
And on the watery satin sheet
of Lake George
A mob of kangaroos sits bolt upright
to greet us ...

Mr. Darwin's room

(National Museum of Australia)

*A man who dares to waste one hour
of time has not discovered the value of
life.* —Charles Darwin

Inside a structure
of rainbow loops and angles
spangle whirling
over a cellophane lake
is Mr. Darwin's room,
exactly as he left it:
cards tucked in the mirror,
pictures on the wall,
a basket by the fire,
unassuming clutter.
And all around the mutter
as foreign children stop and count
his instruments and books
(microscopes and jars)
odd playthings of a lifetime.

Outside ...
a blue untroubled sky
rustles gently in the water
antipodean parrots flit
and settle on the grass—
their ancestors are under glass
inside this unfamiliar place—

and an old man's chair is empty.

Spring day in Kingston

Bare armed girls tilt back
on Van Gogh's yellow chairs,
flouncing petal skirts, under a tint
of new green leaves. Nearby, old women
lift cups to toast the air
and a child sniffs
the potted pinkness of a cyclamen.
Bicycles and prams churn up lemon light
on the sun buttered pavement,
flecking passersby with gold.
Outside the bookshop a student pauses
to dabble in poems and dreams.
Pages unfurl like prayer flags
and a spring breeze ruffles his soft hair.

Poppies

This morning they sat
in a florist's bucket
waving wildly at passersby
(sassy girls in crumpled silk).

She stoops to rearrange their skirts.
The poppies shimmy on undaunted
and we share a glance
over a dance of sunshine, coral and red.

"A party in a vase ..."
I proffer the metaphor shyly
with my loose change.
It hovers between us for a moment
(a tiny gift of words)
then she smiles and reaches out for it
and I put the poppies into my basket.

Luminous miracles

In the dim shade of oak trees
small milky moons erupt
out of the cooling Autumn earth.
Pure white spheres—spattered
incandescent like shot silk—
cerulean, sea green, sapphire,
aqua, jade, verdigris ...
some tattered and frayed
but still smudged with
enamelled shine.
Where have they come from—
these luminous miracles?
Soon they will be gone
and the ground will be dark once more ...
but somewhere deep in the rot
and richness of cold soil—
tangled among roots and insects
are filaments of sky-bright light ...

Vighneshvara: Destroyer of obstacles

(for my father in his time of grief)

I bring you sweets although
I know that you prefer salty food,
but today is a time to bring sweets ...
and so I bring you sweets in a round
bowl—scented with
cardamom and slick with ghee ...
Dip your hand
(like Ganesha's joyful trunk)
into this *modakapatra*,
and hold sunshine and sorrow, the moon
and stars, mountains and skies, love
and despair, hold oceans and rainbows,
anger and hope, hold all the universes
—past, present and future ...
hold the moment when you placed
these same sweets into
my childish mouth (the sparkling crunch
of syrup soaked *jalebi, gulab jamun*
as warm and soft as your eyes,
golden *laddu* and the soothing milkiness of
nut scattered *burfi*)
I bring you sweets at this sad time
of change and loss ...
Do not grieve over your broken tusk
Remember obstacles and heartaches
are placed and removed in the blink
of an elephant's eye—
So dip your trunk into this bowl of sweets
and smile and sigh ...

Nest

In bare branches of the jacaranda tree
two peewees settle and flutter
around the dark cup of their nest
(Are there babies?
It's too hard to see from down here
on the verandah of my parents' house)
the mother bird huddles down cosily
in her tiny home ...
unaware of rustling pages
and the scraping of a chair
on wooden floorboards
as my father reads and remembers
in soft rays of lonely sunshine ...

The last despair

> *They brought her ribbons of yellow and crimson and great clusters of flowers*—Charles Blackman

These ancient bones float light
across the indigo night, this ravaged face
is mollified into the supple sleep
of girlhood, lost thoughts drift free—

I hang gentle ...

Tomorrow they will tidy my scant hair,
paint my lips and lay me out, they will
bring flowers looped in crimson ribbons,
and my best dress to wear ...
Tonight there is only the gentian dark,
golden, gauzy swathes of dreaming and
a pillow of petals to soften the last despair ...

In our great grandmother's room

In our great grandmother's room
tubes of paint have dried
hard as bone—
tiny coffins
too stiff to open—
We brush insect carcasses,
off tantalising labels
Chinese White, Lemon Yellow, Crimson, Ultramarine,
Viridian Green, Ochre, Burnt Umber, Magenta ...
We yearn to squeeze
this brilliance out
in globs and squirts ...
Searching further we find
dishes of dessicated colour—
Later we browse through her
final unfinished canvases—
cobwebs and grime—
then we roll up our paintings
to take home
and quietly, quietly
close the door ...

Bereft

Bereft in every font and size
tapped out
on a salt wet keyboard—
Bereft:
underlined and bolded
in Copperplate, Cambria,
Gothic and Goudy Stout
Bereft:
Gabriola tiny—almost invisible
but suddenly
italicised and coloured red
as the skinned rabbit of my heart—
quivering and turning at every
sound and light—
Bereft:
in Garamond, Castellar and
Déjà vu
in Lucida Calligraphy and
Arial and Century Schoolbook,
in purple Wide Latin size 72 ...
then shrinking slowly,
inevitably back
into the dark finality
of size 12 Calibri black ...

You would have loved the flowers …

You would have loved the flowers
today (no prissy roses or stiff cold
lilies or timid carnations or flimsy daisies)
None of that for you …
You would have loved the spiky
orange and gentian blue of
strelitzia, winging from
polished wood like a blazing bird,
the verdant lushness of monsterio
and the waxy certainty of heart
shaped anthuriums … you would have
loved the sprays of orchids—not too many
but enough to remind us of your
mother's garden—and a few proteas
prickling the glory with their quirky
brightness … all your favourite blooms
and greenness … how you would have
loved to arrange them in bowls and
vases and jugs and urns …

Family tree

Our family tree was
chopped down long ago
(roots ripped up, leaves
and bark crumbled
into the soil of an unknown
place) when a man vanished
without a trace
leaving no footprints
in the dust of his village
(or was it a town?)
bringing nothing—not a single
memory, not a song or story or
word of his language—
arriving without baggage,
photographs or souvenirs ...
planting a new tree in foreign
earth—unencumbered by
past branches—leaving us
with no names to put
in all those empty boxes ...

Pontianak

They say the *Pontianak*,
in the mango tree,
pushed my aunty out of leafy branches—
a spiteful shove—by all accounts—
she fell headlong into the poultry yard,
breaking her arm and
frightening the geese ...
My grandmother ordered that the tree
be chopped down immediately ...
in order to rid the garden of this tragic,
vicious creature—*perempuan mati
beranak*—
waiting to steal her next young victim ...
everyone mourned the end of those
luscious mangoes—the sweetest
in the orchard ... but a female vampire
(who died in childbirth)
must be taken seriously ...
and my grandmother who had
felt the last exhale of soft breath
from three small bodies
—held tight in her arms—
knew that grief for golden fruit
would not last long ...

Afterword

Common garments have always found their way into my poetry—the red sari of a terrified Indian bride, the batik sarong of my Malay ancestors, the pink and white stripes of a breast cancer clinic robe, a pair of blue jeans worn by a skinny, brown teenage girl growing up in 1970s Australia ...

Poems like garments tell the story of our uniqueness and our commonality—they cover and reveal, they obscure the truth and they expose the truth. Like a garment, a poem is painstakingly crafted—each word is chosen with precision and the whole piece is stitched together with care. Honing a poem is a joyful task. There is no place for even a slightly wrong syllable in poetry. Every single word matters.

All of us are wrapped in our stories—in the prosaic and exquisite, in ordinary moments and complex relationships, in our history and our present lives. We are clothed in hope and loss, in happiness and sorrow, in anger and fear, in love and yearning.

We all wear the common garment of humanity.

Notes

'Geragok'

'Geragok' was inspired by reading *The Shrimp People* by Rex Shelley (Times Books International, 1991). *Geragok* is the Malay name for the Portuguese Eurasian or Kristang people of Malaysia. This mixed race traces its ancestry back to around 1500 AD when the first Portuguese sailors arrived on the shores of Malacca and were encouraged to marry Malay women. The word *geragok* also means small shrimp and refers to the fact that the Portuguese Malaccans were traditionally shrimp fishermen. These shrimp dried and pounded with hot chillies are the key ingredient in *sambal belacan* or chilly prawn paste which is fundamental to Malay Eurasian cooking. There is always a small dish of this condiment on the dining table in Kristang homes.

'Raising Ravana'

This poem refers to characters from the great Hindu epic the Ramayana. Ravana is the demon king of Alangka who captured Princess Sita from her husband Rama. Sita was rescued from the kingdom of Alangka (Sri Langka) by Rama with the help of the valiant monkey general Hanuman. In the final battle between good and evil Hanuman sets fire to Ravana's kingdom with his tail. Children in Hindu communities all over the world look forward to the annual festivals of Dasehra and Diwali. During Dasehra the Ramayana is acted publicly and the paper figure of the arch demon Ravana is destroyed in a bonfire. Good triumphs over evil and the return of Rama and Sita from exile is celebrated by Diwali, the festival of lights.

'Navigating Gija Country'

Thank you to the Gija Artists of Western Australia, the Warmun Art Centre and Nancy Sever Gallery for bringing this astonishing country to Canberra.

'Dia'

The pronoun dia means he, she, his and hers in Bahasa Indonesia and Malay.

'That's their story'

Kali is a Dravidian Indus goddess (from the ancient Indian pre Aryan pantheon). She is well over 2000 years old. She embodies the essence of female energy (Shakti). She is thought of as the great mother goddess, the darkness from which all life springs. Kali is usually depicted as naked, blue black, blood-thirsty, and wild-haired. With the arrival of the Aryan patriarchal pantheon the stories around Kali changed. One of those changed stories tells of how Kali fought and killed some demons. After her victory she was so elated that she started the dance of death. Nothing could calm her and so her husband Lord Shiva had to intervene. He threw himself amongst the bodies of slain demons. Kali was forced to look down and found Shiva there. She snapped out of her reverie and became extremely ashamed and regretful.

'Sita'

Sita, the wife of Rama, is the principal female character in the *Ramayana*, an Indian epic which underpins Hinduism and is the oldest written story in the world. When Rama is banished to the forest for fourteen years instead of being crowned king, Sita insists on going with him. They live happily in the forest until Sita is captured by a demon king named Ravana. Rama and his brother Laksmana set out to rescue her. Rama and Laksmana eventually rescue Sita, with the help of an army of monkeys, but Rama doubts Sita's purity, after the time she has spent in Ravana's kingdom. Sita endures a trial by fire and proves herself untouched by any but Rama. They return home and Rama becomes king, but she becomes the subject of street gossip, so he banishes her to the forest. In the final chapter of the *Ramayana*, when Rama comes to take Sita back with him, she does not meekly submit but chooses her own fate. She chooses to return to the earth, instead of remaining with a man who has twice abandoned her. This poem offers Sita's perspective in a story that has traditionally been completely centered around the male protagonist, Rama.

'Vighneshvara: Destroyer of Obstacles'

The Hindu god Ganesha (a beloved elephant headed deity riding a mouse) is the son of Lord Shiva and goddess Parvati. He is revered as the Lord of Beginnings and the Destroyer of Obstacles—Vighneshvara. He is depicted with a broken tusk and holding various sacred symbolic objects including a bowl of sweets.

Acknowledgements

Many thanks to the editors of the following publications where versions of these poems first appeared:

'Tsunami' and 'Raising Ravana' in *Conversations* (Pandanus Press, ANU), Vol 6 Number 2 Summer 2006

'Women's Talk' in *Block* Issue 9

'Poppies' and 'Mr. Darwin's room' in *Burley* Issue One May 2012

'Peribahasa', 'Don't Be Afraid *(Jangan Merasa Takut)*' and 'Soul' in *Demos Journal* Issue 5 Resistance October 21, 2016

'Apples and Chillies' and 'So Much Fruit' in *Mascara Literary Review*, March 21, 2017

'Fried Bread and Mango Juice' in *Cordite Poetry Review* 86: NO THEME VII, May 1, 2018

'Mr. Darwin's room', 'Wajah/Muka', 'Cane Cutter's Bride' and 'Women's Talk' in States of Poetry Series Three—ACT Australian Book Review June 2018

'Surat Udara (Aerogramme)' in *Pink Cover Zine* Issue 3, 'Mementos' September 2018

'colours of her country' and 'Navigating Gija Country' in *Not Very Quiet Journal*, Issue 3, September, 2018

'Sita' in *FemAsia Magazine* 25 October 2018

'Aunties', 'Soul', 'Makan Angin (Eating the Air)' and 'Poppies' in *Not Very Quiet Journal*, Issue 2, Guest Editor's Profile, March 2018

'Women's Talk', Winner, the ACT Writers' Centre Poetry Prize 2004

My profound thanks to Shane Strange, publisher of Recent Work Press, for being such a skilled editor and supportive friend. Thank you also to Niloofar Fanaiyan, Moya Pacey, Sandra Renew and Jen Webb who have offered me valuable advice, wonderful opportunities and so much kindness. I am honoured to have these generous poets as my friends. Thanks to the organisers of That Poetry Thing at Smith's - an event which gives us a chance to hear the work of emerging and established poets in a splendid venue every week.

My gratitude to the *Canberra Times* for publishing my early poems many years ago and giving me some hope of becoming a real poet.

I want to pay tribute to my parents who nourished me with words, food and love and who gave me my first stories.

Finally, a huge and loving thank you to my husband, Scott, and to my children who have lived with my poetry through thick and thin and always believed in me.

About the author

Anita Patel has had work published in the *Canberra Times*, in *Conversations (Pandanus Press, ANU)*, in *Block 9, Burley Journal, Cha: An Asian Literary Journal, Demos Journal, Mascara Literary Review, Not Very Quiet Journal, Cordite Poetry Review, Backstory Journal, Other Terrain Journal, Pink Cover Zine, FemAsia Magazine and Eucalypt: a tanka journal*. Her children's poems are included in an anthology *Pardon My Garden* published by Harper Collins. Her poem "Women's Talk" won the ACT Writers Centre Poetry Prize in 2004 and her poetry was selected for and published in Australian Book Review's States of Poetry ACT, 2018.

She has performed her work at the Canberra Multicultural Festival, Poetry on the Move Festival, Noted Festival, Floriade Fringe Festival, In Other Words Festival (at Lost in Books, Fairfield), the Queensland Poetry Festival, the National Folk Festival, at Smith's Alternative and at Word in Hand, Glebe.

Her reviews, 'Found in Translation', on the performances of four Japanese women poets and their translators at Poetry on the Move Festival, 2017 and 'No More Silent Waiting', on the anthology *Autonomy* edited by Kathy D'Arcy (2018) have been published by *Not Very Quiet Journal*. She was the guest editor for Issue 2 of *Not Very Quiet Journal*.

2019 Editions

Palace of Memory: An elegy **Paul Hetherington**
Acting Like a Girl **Sandra Renew**
A Coat of Ashes **Jackson**
Summer Haiku **Owen Bullock**
A Common Garment **Anita Patel**
Strange Stars: A Queer Poetry Anthology **Various**
Giant Steps **Various**
Some Sketchy Notes on Matter **Angela Gardner**
The Question Nest **Peter Bakowski**
Breathing in Stormy Seasons **Stephanie Green**
Strange Creatures **Alyson Miller**

2018 Editions

The Uncommon Feast **Eileen Chong**
Inlandia **KA Nelson**
Peripheral Vision **Martin Dolan**
The Love of the Sun **Matt Hetherington**
Moving Targets **Jen Webb**
Things I Have Thought to Tell You Since I Saw You Last **Penelope Layland**
The Many Uses of Mint **Ravi Shankar**
Abstractions **Various**
ACE: Arresting, Contemporary stories by Emerging Writers **Various**

all titles available from

www.recentworkpress.com

www.ingramcontent.com/pod-product-compliance
Lightning Source LLC
Chambersburg PA
CBHW032049290426
44110CB00012B/1022